States
TENNESSEE

by Bridget Parker

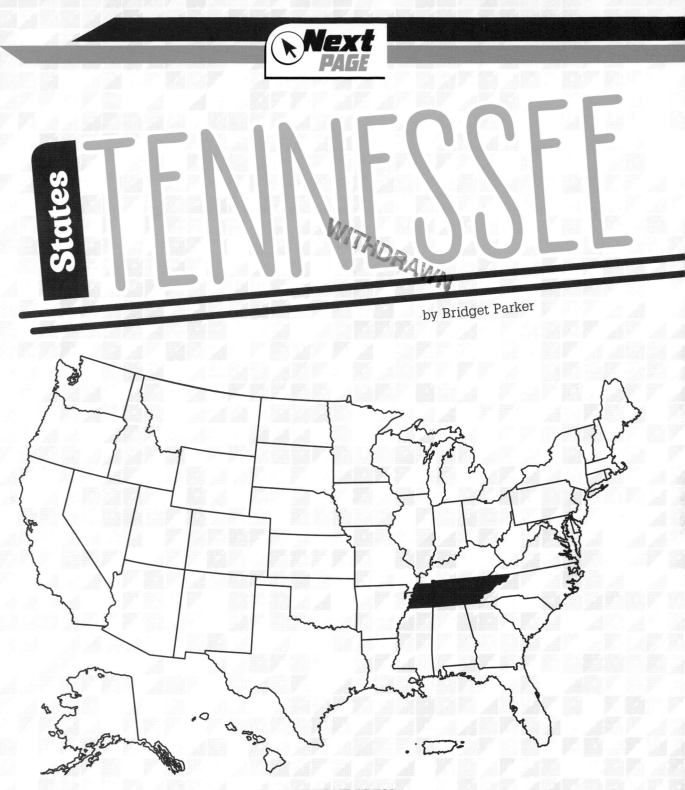

CAPSTONE PRESS
a capstone imprint

Next Page Books are published by Capstone Press,
1710 Roe Crest Drive, North Mankato, Minnesota 56003
www.mycapstone.com

Library of Congress Cataloging-in-Publication Data
Cataloging-in-publication information is on file with the Library of
Congress.
ISBN 978-1-5157-0430-0 (library binding)
ISBN 978-1-5157-0489-8 (paperback)
ISBN 978-1-5157-0541-3 (ebook PDF)

Editorial Credits
Jaclyn Jaycox, editor; Kazuko Collins and Katy LaVigne, designers;
Morgan Walters, media researcher; Tori Abraham, production specialist

Photo Credits
Capstone Press: Angi Gahler, map 4, 7; CriaImages.com: Jay Robert
Nash Collection, top 18, middle 19; Dreamstime: Clewisleake, 17,
Karenfoleyphotography, 11; Getty Images: National Geographic/
Stephen Alvarez, middle left 21; Karipearls.com, top left 21; Newscom:
Album / Oronoz, 12, BILLY WEEKS/Reuters, 14; North Wind Picture
Archives, 25; One Mile Up, Inc., flag, seal 23; Shutterstock: A.H.
Bishop Photography, bottom right 8, aceshot1, 15, Action Sports
Photography, bottom 24, almondd, 10, Blulz60, bottom right 21, Bonita
R. Cheshier, 16, Brian Dunne, 9, Carla Donofrio, 29, cinemafestival,
bottom 19, Creative Jen Designs, 27, cristalvi, top left 20, Dave
Newman, 13, Elizabeth Cronin, bottom left 21, f11photo, 5, Helga
Esteb, bottom 18, IgorGolovniov, 28, Jason Patrick Ross, top right 21,
Jill Nightingale, bottom left 20, Juice Team, top right 20, Kenneth
Sponsler, 7, KennStilger47, top 24, Malgorzata Litkowska, 26, Melinda
Fawver, bottom left 8, s_bukley, middle 18, Sean Pavone, cover, Sergey
Goryachev, top 19, Songquan Deng, middle right 21, Teri and Jackie
Soares, bottom right 20, Zack Frank, 6

All design elements by Shutterstock

Printed and bound in China.
0316/CA21600187
012016   009436F16

TABLE OF CONTENTS

Want to take your research further? Ask your librarian if your school subscribes to PebbleGo Next. If so, when you see this helpful symbol ⊕ throughout the book, log onto www.pebblegonext.com for bonus downloads and information.

LOCATION

Tennessee is in the southeastern United States. Eight other states border Tennessee. Kentucky and Virginia are Tennessee's northern neighbors. Three neighbors lie to the south—Georgia, Alabama, and Mississippi. North Carolina is the only neighbor east of Tennessee. To the west are Missouri and Arkansas. Nashville, the capital, is in the middle of the state. Tennessee's largest cities are Nashville, Memphis, and Knoxville.

PebbleGo Next Bonus!
To print and label your own map, go to www.pebblegonext.com and search keywords:
TN MAP

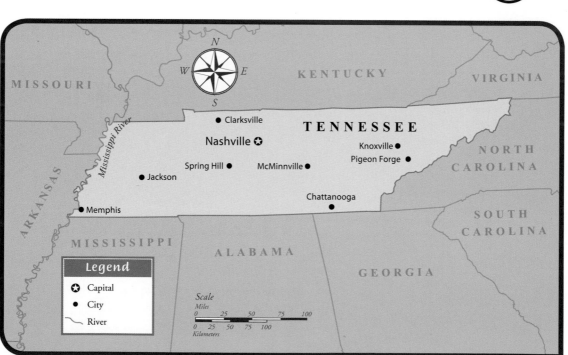

Nashville, also known as "Music City," is home to more than 650,000 people.

GEOGRAPHY

Tennessee has three land regions. They are East, Middle, and West Tennessee. The Unaka, Great Smoky, and Cumberland Mountains lie in the East region. These ranges are part of the Appalachians. A low, flat area called the Central Basin makes up Middle Tennessee. The Tennessee River encircles the basin. The Mississippi River and the Great Central Plain are in the West. In the East region, Tennessee's highest point, Clingmans Dome, is in Great Smoky Mountain National Park. This mountain peak rises 6,643 feet (2,025 meters) above sea level.

PebbleGo Next Bonus! To watch a video about the Country Music Hall of Fame, go to www.pebblegonext.com and search keywords:

TN VIDEO

Calderwood Lake is located in eastern Tennessee.

Tennessee, Kentucky, and Viginia all meet at the Cumberland Gap.

N
W   E
S

Mississippi River

Reelfoot Lake

GULF COASTAL PLAIN

LAND BETWEEN THE LAKES NATIONAL RECREATION AREA

Tennessee River

HIGHLAND RIM CENTRAL BASIN

BIG SOUTH FORK NATIONAL RIVER AND RECREATION AREA

CUMBERLAND MOUNTAINS

Cumberland Gap

GREAT VALLEY

APPALACHIAN MOUNTAINS

Clingmans Dome

GREAT SMOKY MOUNTAINS NATIONAL PARK

Scale
Miles
0   25   50   75   100
0 25 50 75 100
Kilometers

Legend

▲ Highest Point

⬡ Lake

⛰ Mountain Range

⬛ National Park or Recreation Area

○ Point of Interest

〰 River

WEATHER

Tennessee's climate is mild. In summer the temperature averages 76 degrees Fahrenheit (24 degrees Celsius). Winters in Tennessee have an average temperature of 39°F (4°C).

Average High and Low Temperatures (Memphis, TN)

Month	High	Low
JAN	50	33
FEB	55	36
MAR	64	44
APR	73	53
MAY	81	62
JUN	89	70
JUL	92	74
AUG	91	73
SEP	85	65
OCT	74	54
NOV	63	44
DEC	52	35

LANDMARKS

Great Smoky Mountains National Park

Great Smoky Mountains is America's most visited national park. More than 9 million visitors enter the park each year to see the beautiful mountain scenery.

Sunsphere

The Sunsphere in Knoxville was built for the World's Fair in 1982. This steel structure is 266 feet (81 m) tall.

Beale Street Historic District

Beale Street in downtown Memphis is the birthplace of blues music. The Beale Street Music Festival takes place every year in May.

HISTORY AND GOVERNMENT

Daniel Boone leads settlers through the Cumberland Gap.

In the mid-1500s, the first Europeans arrived in Tennessee. Frenchmen Louis Jolliet and Jacques Marquette came to Tennessee in 1673 to trade with American Indians for furs. European settlers had difficulty moving to the Tennessee region. In March 1775 Daniel Boone led a group of men to blaze a trail across the Appalachians through the Cumberland Gap. During the Revolutionary War (1775–1783), American colonists fought against Great Britain for their independence. Settlers in Tennessee helped the colonies fight. In 1796 Tennessee became the 16th state.

The Tennessee state government includes the executive, legislative, and judicial branches. The executive branch carries out laws. The legislative branch is known as the General Assembly. This branch suggests and makes laws. It includes 33 members in the Senate and 99 members in the House of Representatives. The judicial branch is made up of all the courts in the state.

The architect of the Tennessee state capitol, William Strickland, is buried within the walls of the building.

INDUSTRY

Tennessee factories produce a wide variety of products. Car manufacturing is one of Tennessee's most important industries. Tennessee factories also produce computers, aircraft, and industrial chemicals. The state is one of the nation's leading producers of wood products from oak, walnut, and hickory trees.

Music is a major part of the tourism industry in Tennessee. Many recording studios are located in Memphis and Nashville.

Of Tennessee's 95 counties, 88 of them have automotive operations. This industry employs more than 105,000 people.

Agriculture is an important part of the state's industry. Tobacco and cotton are two of the state's most important crops. Other top agricultural products include beef cattle, dairy products, and poultry. Tennessee is also famous for its horses. Many people in the state raise horses on large farms.

The Grand Ole Opry in Nashville was founded in 1925.

POPULATION

Many Europeans came to Tennessee from Italy, Ireland, Scotland, and Germany. They make up part of the state's 5 million people who are of European descent. More than 16 percent of Tennesseans are African-Americans. Compared to many other states, few Tennesseans are Asian, Hispanic, or American Indian. About 60 percent of Tennesseans live in or near the state's largest cities, such as Memphis, Nashville, Knoxville, and Chattanooga.

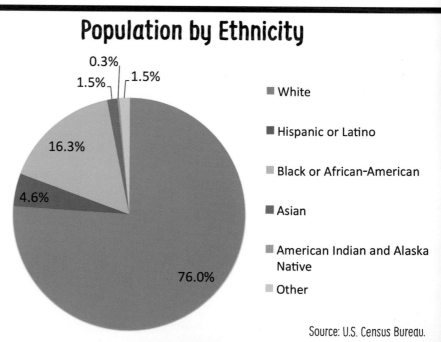

Population by Ethnicity

0.3%
1.5%
1.5%
16.3%
4.6%
76.0%

- White
- Hispanic or Latino
- Black or African-American
- Asian
- American Indian and Alaska Native
- Other

Source: U.S. Census Bureau.

FAMOUS PEOPLE

Davy Crockett (1786–1836) was an expert in frontier living. He was a U.S. congressman from Tennessee (1827–1831 and 1833–1835). He died in the Battle of the Alamo in 1836, fighting for Texas against Mexico.

Al Gore (1948–) is a former U.S. senator (1985–1992) from Tennessee. He served as vice president under President Bill Clinton (1993–2001). He lost the 2000 presidential election to George W. Bush.

Dolly Parton (1946–) is a beloved country music singer and songwriter. Dollywood, a theme park, is near Pigeon Forge.

Elvis Presley (1935–1977) is called the "King of Rock and Roll." Graceland, Presley's home in Memphis, is now a museum.

Sequoyah (circa 1775–1843), a Cherokee Indian, created an alphabet for the Cherokee language. He is the only person in history to develop an alphabet by himself.

Justin Timberlake (1981–) is a Grammy Award–winning singer and performer. A member of the popular band NSYNC in the late 1990s, he has gone on to have a successful solo career. He was born in Memphis.

STATE SYMBOLS

tulip tree

iris

mockingbird

Tennessee walking horse

PebbleGo Next Bonus! To make a dessert using one of Tennessee's top-produced fruits, go to www.pebblegonext.com and search keywords: **TN RECIPE**

Gemstone

Tennessee River pearls

Reptile

eastern box turtle

Amphibian

Tennessee cave salamander

Animal

raccoon

Butterfly

zebra swallowtail

Folk Dance

square dance

FAST FACTS

STATEHOOD
1796

CAPITAL ☆
Nashville

LARGEST CITY •
Memphis

SIZE
41,235 square miles (106,798 square kilometers) land area
(2010 U.S. Census Bureau)

POPULATION
6,495,978 (2013 U.S. Census estimate)

STATE NICKNAME
Volunteer State, Big Bend State

STATE MOTTO
"Agriculture and Commerce"

STATE SEAL

Tennessee's state seal was adopted in 1987. The Roman numeral XVI at the top of the seal shows that Tennessee was the 16th state. The upper half of the seal features a plow, a bundle of wheat, and a cotton plant. These items stand for agriculture. A ship is at the bottom of the seal. It represents the trade of Tennessee's goods with others.

PebbleGo Next Bonus! To print and color your own flag, go to www.pebblegonext.com and search keywords:

TN FLAG

STATE FLAG

Tennessee's legislature adopted the state flag in 1905. It has a red background. A blue circle with a white border is in the center of the flag. Three white stars are in the middle of the circle. Each star stands for one of the state's regions, East, Middle, and West Tennessee. One thin white stripe and a blue stripe are on the flag's right side.

MINING PRODUCTS
limestone, clay, gemstones

MANUFACTURED GOODS
tobacco, chemicals, motor vehicle parts, machinery, computer parts and electrical equipment, wood products

FARM PRODUCTS
tobacco, cotton, soybeans, corn, wheat

PROFESSIONAL SPORTS TEAMS
Memphis Grizzlies (NBA)
Nashville Predators (NHL)
Tennessee Titans (NFL)

PebbleGo Next Bonus!
To learn the lyrics to the state song, go to www.pebblegonext.com and search keywords:

TN SONG

TENNESSEE TIMELINE

1540 Hernando de Soto explores Tennessee; at the time, Cherokee, Chickasaw, Creek, and Shawnee Indian nations are living in Tennessee.

1620 The Pilgrims establish a colony in the New World in present-day Massachusetts.

1772 Small groups of British colonists settle in eastern Tennessee and form the Watauga Association.

1775 Daniel Boone establishes a trail through the Appalachians that was later renamed the Wilderness Road; thousands of settlers begin traveling to the Kentucky and Tennessee areas.

**1796**   Tennessee becomes the 16th state on June 1.

1811–1812   Earthquakes strike Tennessee, causing land in the northwestern part of the state to sink and form Reelfoot Lake.

1861–1865   The Union and the Confederacy fight the Civil War. Tennessee fights on the side of the Confederacy.

1914–1918   World War I is fought; the United States enters the war in 1917.

1933
The U.S. Congress forms the Tennessee Valley Authority to manage natural resources and provide electricity to the region.

1939–1945
World War II is fought; the United States enters the war in 1941.

1955
The Grand Ole Opry begins television broadcasts.

1960
Students hold sit-in demonstrations at Nashville lunch counters.

 **1968** On April 4 Martin Luther King Jr., a supporter of civil rights, is murdered in Memphis.

 **1982** The World's Fair is held in Knoxville.

USA 20c

Synthetic fuels Knoxville World's Fair

 **1985** General Motors opens a new assembly plant for Saturn cars in Spring Hill.

 **1993** On January 20 Al Gore becomes vice president of the United States. Gore is from Carthage.

2003 On May 4, 11 people are killed by tornadoes in Jackson.

2010 In May, torrential rain causes the Cumberland River to flood in Nashville; 11 people die.

2015 The Department of Developmental and Intellectual Disabilities' state service delivery system receives accreditation, which is the first in the country.

Glossary

broadcast *(BRAHD-kast)*—to send out a program on TV

demonstrate *(DEM-uhn-strayt)*—to join together with others to protest something

encircle *(en-SUR-kuhl)*—to form a circle around

executive *(ig-ZE-kyuh-tiv)*—the branch of government that makes sure laws are followed

frontier *(furhn-TIHR)*—the far edge of a settled area, where few people live

industry *(IN-duh-stree)*—a business which produces a product or provides a service

judicial (joo-DISH-uhl)—to do with the branch of government that explains and interprets the laws

legislature *(LEJ-iss-lay-chur)*—a group of elected officials who have the power to make or change laws for a country or state

torrential *(TOR-uhn-shuhl)*—a large amount of water that is released suddenly

tourism *(TOOR-i-zuhm)*—the business of taking care of visitors to a country or place

volunteer *(vol-uhn-TIHR)*—a person who chooses to do work without pay

Read More

Ganeri, Anita. *United States of America: A Benjamin Blog and His Inquisitive Dog Guide.* Country Guides. Chicago: Heinemann Raintree Library, 2015.

Petreycik, Rick, and William McGeveran. *Tennessee.* It's My State! New York: Cavendish Square, 2014.

VanVoorst, Jenny Fretland. *What's Great About Tennessee?* Our Great States. Minneapolis: Lerner Publications Company, 2015.

Internet Sites

FactHound offers a safe, fun way to find Internet sites related to this book. All of the sites on FactHound have been researched by our staff.

Here's all you do:

Visit *www.facthound.com*

Type in this code: 9781515704300

 Check out projects, games and lots more at
www.capstonekids.com

Critical Thinking Using the Common Core

1. Look at the map on page 4. Which states border Tennessee? (Craft and Structure)

2. What are the three land regions that make up Tennessee? (Key Ideas and Details)

3. The upper half of Tennessee's state seal represents agriculture. What is depicted on this part of the seal? (Key Ideas and Details)

Index